JOKES

POCKET-SIZED

Copyright © 2019 by Stanley Singer

All rights reserved. No part of this publication may be reproduced, distributed, or transmitted in any form or by any means, including photocopying, recording, or other electronic or mechanical methods, without the prior written permission of the publisher, except in the case of brief quotations embodied in critical reviews and certain other noncommercial uses permitted by copyright law.

Why did the little boy run away
while making pancakes?
**Because the instructions said,
"Crack an egg then beat it!"**

Why are pirates so mean?
They just arrrrr!

Why don't you see giraffes in
elementary school?
Because they're all in high school!

Who invented King Arthur's round table?
Sir Circumference!

Why was the boy scout such a good racecar driver?
Because he did a good turn daily!

What do you call a dinosaur with an extensive vocabulary?
A thesaurus.

What happened when the cows escaped the ranch?
Udder chaos!

Why was the basketball arena hot after the game?
Because all the fans had left!

Why did Cinderella get kicked off the soccer team?
Because she kept running away from the ball.

Why does Dracula's wife have trouble sleeping at night?
Because of his coffin.

Did you hear about the Italian chef that died?
He pasta way.

Knock Knock
Who's there?
Mansion!
Mansion who?
Did I mansion I have a big house?

What do toads like to drink on a cold day?
Hot croako!

What kind of music did the Pilgrims like?
Plymouth Rock.

If April showers bring May flowers, what do May flowers bring?
Pilgrims.

Why can't you take a turkey to church?
They use fowl language.

How can you help a fish with its singing?
Autotuna.

Why do fish always know how much they weigh?
Because they have their own scales.

What does an agreeable pickle always say?
"I relish the idea."

What is the best way to carve wood?
Whittle by whittle!

What did the astronaut cook in his skillet?
Unidentified frying objects.

Where do polar bears vote?
The North Poll.

What do farmers give their wives at midnight on New Year's Eve?
Hogs and kisses!

Why did the turtle cross the road?
To get to the Shell Station.

Why did Mickey Mouse go into outer space?
To see Pluto.

How does a bee get to class?
On the school-buzz.

What do chickens grow on?
Eggplants!

Why were the dark ages so dark?
Because there were so many knights.

Why did the man put a clock under his desk?
Because he wanted to work over-time!

Did you hear about the wig factory truck that crashed?
Police are still combing the area!

What do you get when you play tug-of-war with a pig?
Pulled pork.

Why are elephants so wrinkled?
They're too hard to iron.

What did the pig say when he was sick?
"Call the ham-bulance!"

Where do fish go to do yoga?
The river bend.

What did the duck say when she bought a lipstick?
"Put it on my bill!"

What do you call a sleeping egg?
Egg-zosted!

What do farmers need to create crop circles?
A pro-tractor.

What are the rules in zebra baseball?
Three stripes and you're out!

How do you make an octopus laugh?
With ten-tickles!

Why don't mummies go on vacation?
Because they are afraid to relax and unwind.

How did the basketball get all wet?
The players dribbled all over it.

What did the band say when they were asked to play classical music?
"I don't think we can Handel it."

What's a pig's best karate move?
The pork chop!

What is a duck's favorite video game?
Quack-man!

How do you cut the ocean in half?
With a sea saw!

Why couldn't anyone see the bird?
Because it was in da skies!

Does the Easter Bunny like baseball?
Oh, yes. He's a rabbit fan!

Do you like Civil War Jokes?
Because General Lee I don't find them funny.

How does a dog stop a video?
By pressing the paws button.

What is a lion's favorite food?
Baked beings!

What is purple and super long?
The Grape Wall of China.

What do you get when you run behind a car?
Exhausted.

Why did the computer go to the doctor?
Because it had a virus!

Did you hear about the two bed bugs who met in the mattress?
They got married in the spring.

Why did Captain Hook get suspended from school?
For playing hooky.

What has 18 legs and catches flies?
A baseball team!

What do you call a fly with no wings?
A "walk!"

What do you call a flower that runs on electricity?
A power plant.

What do you get when you put four ducks in a box?
A box of quackers!

What did the alien say to the garden?
"Take me to your weeder!"

I forgot how to throw a boomerang
but then
it came back to me!

Why did the clam work out?
Because it wanted mussels.

What do chickens study in school?
Eggonomics.

What is a dog's favorite breakfast?
Pooched eggs!

What kind of shoes do frogs wear?
Open toad!

What did the sushi say to the rice?
"Wasabi!"

Where do ghosts like to go swimming?
Lake Eerie.

Which month do soldiers hate most?
March!

Did you hear the joke about the roof?
Never mind, it's over your head.

What did the cannibal get when he was late for dinner?
A cold shoulder.

Knock Knock!
Who's there?
Isma
Isma who?
Isma lunch ready yet?

What's a tornado's favorite food?
Funnel cake.

What did the snowman and his wife hang over their baby's crib?
A snow mobile.

What did the bunny give his girlfriend when he asked her to marry him?
A 14-carrot ring!

What do you call a computer that sings with powerful voice?
A-Dell.

Why was the baby ant confused?
Because all its uncles were ants.

What would a reindeer do if it lost its tail?
It would go to the "re-tail" shop for a new one!

Why did the veggie band sound horrible?
They were missing a beet.

Knock Knock.
Who's there?
Rupert!
Rupert who?
Rupert your left foot in, Rupert your left foot out, Rupert your left foot in and you shake it all about...

How does Reese eat her ice cream?
Witherspoon.

What's a cow's favorite painting?
The Moona Lisa.

Why was the scalene triangle sad?
He would never be right.

Why did the spider take swimming lessons?
He wanted to surf the Web.

Why do sharks swim in salt water?
Because pepper water makes them sneeze.

What do fish need to stay healthy?
Vitamin Sea.

What do you call a reindeer with no eyes?
No eye deer.

Why did the oyster take all the food for itself?
It was shellfish.

What did the bee to the other bee in summertime?
"Swarm in here, isn't it!"

Why did the music teacher need a ladder?
To reach the high notes.

What is a queen's favorite kind of weather?
Reign!

Where did the seaweed find a job?
In the kelp-wanted section.

What do sea monsters eat?
Fish and ships!

What kind of tea did the American colonists like?
Liberty.

What did Beethoven do when he died?
He decomposed!

How does a man on a moon get his haircut?
Eclipse it.

What did Obi-Wan say at the rodeo?
"Use the horse, Luke!"

Why did the boy bury his flashlight?
Because the batteries died.

Why did the spotted cat get disqualified from the race?
It was a cheetah.

What is a zombie's favorite football team?
The Washington Deadskins!

Why doesn't anybody like Dracula?
He has a bat temper.

What is a kangaroo's favorite season?
Spring!

What do you get if you cross a sports reporter with a vegetable?
A common tater!

Knock Knock
Who's there?
Zeroes!
Zeroes who?
**Zeroes zeroes as fast as she can,
but she still lost the boat race.**

Where do you find a birthday present for a cat?
In a cat-alog!

What kind of music are balloons afraid of?
Pop music.

What do you call a wasp?
A wanna-bee!

What is a scarecrow's favorite fruit?
Strawberries!

What are chefs always trying the win?
The Hunger Games.

What do vegetarian zombies crave?
GRAAAINS.....

What is the pickle's philosophy of life?
Never a dill moment.

How do you tie things in space?
With astro-knots.

What did the pig say when it sat in the sun too long?
"I'm bacon!"

What vacation destination makes your pet bird very happy?
The Canary Islands!

What did the corn say when he got complimented?
"Aww, shucks!"

Where do mummies go for a swim?
To the Dead Sea.

How do crazy people go through the forest?
They take the psycho path.

What did the shark say to the whale?
"What are you blubbering about?"

What do you get when you cross a cow and a whale?
Sha-Moo.

How are a dog and a marine biologist alike?
One wags a tail and the other tags a whale.

Why were Serena Williams's neighbors angry?
Because she made a big racquet.

Why did the king go to the dentist?
To get his teeth crowned!

What store can you find horses at?
At Old Neigh-vy

Why didn't the skunk call his parents?
Because his phone was out of odor!

Where did the goblin throw the football?
Over the ghoul line.

What is a smart bird's favorite type of math?
Owl-gebra.

Why did the man quit his job at the bakery?
It was a crumby place to work.

How can you tell when a bank becomes bored?
When it starts losing interest!

Where does a chess player trade in his pieces?
At the pawn shop.

Where are the Great Plains located?
At the great airports!

What did the mama turkey say to her naughty son?
"If your papa could see you now, he'd turn over in his gravy!"

Why are frogs great outfielders?
They never miss a fly.

How can you make a horst fast?
Don't give him anything to eat.

What do you call a lazy baby kangaroo?
A pouch potato!

What is a bird's favorite Christmas story?
The Finch Who Stole Christmas.

Why was the jack-o-lantern afraid to cross the road?
It had no guts!

What did the hungry Dalmatian say when it finished its dinner?
"Boy, that hit the spots!"

What type of movie is about water fowl?
A duckumentary.

Which bird is always out of breath?
A puffin!

Why don't bears like fast food?
Because they can't catch it!

What happened when the farmer crossed a chili pepper, a shovel, and a poodle?
He got a hot-diggity-dog.

Knock Knock
Who's there?
Carson
Carson who?
Carson in school is not allowed!

What do fireflies eat at a restraint?
A light meal.

What did the mother rope say to her child?
"Don't be knotty."

What do you call a rock star who owns a towing company?
"Van-Haulin!"

What did the werewolf eat after he'd had his teeth taken out?
The dentist.

How many birds does it take to change a light bulb?
Toucan do it.

What do polar bears like to eat in the cold?
A brrr-grrr!

What do you call it when a prisoner takes his own mug shot?
A cell-fie.

What is a golfer's favorite lunch?
A ham sand-wedge.

How do chimps get down the stairs?
They slide down the banana-ster!

Where's a mathematician's favorite place to visit?
Times Square.

What did the mathematician say when he lost his parrot?
"Where's my Polly-gon?"

How do people swimming in the ocean say "hi" to each other?
They wave!

What do pigs get when they're ill?
Oinkment!

What do you call a famous turtle?
A shellebrity.

What did the snail say while it was riding on top of the turtle?
"WHEEEEEE!"

Where do fortune tellers dance?
At the crystal ball.

Why should a bowling alley be quiet?
So you can hear a pin drop!

What do you call an iPhone that isn't kidding around?
Dead Siri-ous.

What quacks, has webbed feet, and betrays his country?
Beneduck Arnold.

Why can you never trust spiders?
Because they post stuff on the web.

How do you fix a broken tomato?
Tomato paste!

What do you call two banana peels on the floor?
A pair of slippers.

Why did the ice cream truck break down?
Because of the Rocky Road.

What's the difference between a guitar and a fish?
You can't tuna fish.

What do you call a sheep covered in chocolate?
A Hershey baa.

Why did the obtuse angle go to the beach?
Because it was over 90 degrees.

Why did the elephants get kicked out of the pool?
Because their trunks kept on falling down!

How do trees get on the Internet?
They log in!

What did the Himalayan mountain guide say to his father when he asked him to do something?
"Sher-pa!"

What do you call an alligator in a vest?
An Investigator.

What did the mama buffalo say to
the baby buffalo?
"Bison."

Why was the sedimentary rock
extra cheap?
Because it was on shale.

What is an eagle's favorite
competition?
A talon show.

What happens when you put nutella on salmon?
You get salmonella.

What did the magician say to the fisherman?
"Pick a cod, any cod!"

Why is turtle wax so expensive?
Because their ears are so small!

What do you call an egg from outer space?
An "Egg-stra terrestial".

Why did the scarecrow win the prize?
Because he was outstanding in his field.

What do you call having your grandma on speed dial?
Instagram.

What did the man say to his dead lawnmower?
"Rust in peace."

Did you hear about the kidnapping?
He woke up.

What do you call a bird that flies into a fan?
Shredded tweet.

What do cows tell each other at bedtime?
Dairy tales.

Why did he man only buy nine racquets?
'Cause tennis too many.

What do you call a school that specializes in teaching nuts?
Macademia.

How do you resuscitate a sheep?
You give it Sheep PR.

How do snakes separate bath towels?
Hiss and hers.

What do you call a guy who takes his girlfriend to an ice rink with a half-priced ticket?
A cheapskate.

In what state can you see a priest sneeze and then sit down?
Mass-achu-setts.

Why is the word "dark" spelled with a "k" and not a "c"?
Because you can't c in the dark.

What do you call an Italian Jedi?
Obi-Wan Cannoli.

What do you call a person who lives in Sweden but isn't from there?
An artificial Swedener.

What do you yell at Edgar Allen Poe before he runs into a tree?
"Poetry!"

How long should a jousting match last?
Until knight fall.

What do you call a man who can identify different types of flames?
A fire distinguisher.

What do you call bears with no ears?
B.

What do you call hens stacked up above one another in cages?
Layers.

Why can't T-Rex clap with his hands?
Because he's extinct.

What do you call an organization that donates places to sit?
A chair-ity.

What do you call a sleeping policeman?
An under-covers cop.

Someone who tends to chickens...is
a real-life chicken tender.

What did the sofa say when it got hurt?
"Couch!"

What do you call a man who can't stand?
Neil.

What did the bandleader call his twin daughters?
Anna One, Anna Two...

What do you call a priest who becomes a lawyer?
Father-in-law.

How many vampires are in this room?
I don't know, I can't Count Draculas.

How did the intruder get into the garage?
Intru-da window!

What do you call a row of people lifting a block of cheddar?
A cheesy pickup line.

What should you always split a taxi cab fee?
It's only fare.

What happened to the egg when he was tickled too much?
He cracked up.

What do people who have a phobia of sausages and pessimists have in common?
They both fear the wurst!

Why does Superman get invited to dinners?
Because he's a supperhero.

How did I get out of Iraq?
Iran!

How do locomotives know where to go?
Lots of training.

What do you call an escaped prisoner camping in the woods?
Criminal in tent.

What do you call a cow that is experiencing something from the past?
Deja Moo.

What's TSA called in Canada?
TS, eh?

What types of explorers never seem to get angry?
Nomads.

How do fish go to war?
In tanks!

What do you call a camel with no humps?
Humphrey.

Why is the scarecrow good at his job?
Hay. It's in his jeans!

What do you call a fist bump in the United Kingdom?
A British pound.

What do you call a man with 10 ants?
A landlord.

Did you hear about the mosquito who became a comedian?
They think he's malarious.

What is leather great for sneaking around?
Because it's made of hide.

Why did the man get arrested at the grocery store?
He was disturbing the peas.

What do you get if you cross a centipede and a parrot?
A walkie-talkie.

What do you call the president of a waterproof clothing company?
The head poncho.

How many eyes does cyclops have?
None if you're spelling it correctly.

Did you hear the jokes about the undelivered letters?
No one seems to get them.

What vegetable do plumbers hate?
Leeks.

How many bones are in the human hand?
Just a handful.

What did one pumpkin say to the other?
"Well, hello there, gourd-geous!"

What did the bored scientist do after watching the earth turn for 24 hours?
He called it a day.

What happens when more bullies enroll in school?
The mean goes up.

What's blue and not really heavy at all?
Light blue.

Why can't children tell dad jokes?
They're not full groan.